More
Bloody
Clerihews

More
Bloody
Clerihews

edited by
George Szirtes and
Andy Jackson

Smokestack Books 2022
1 Lake Terrace, Grewelthorpe
Ripon HG4 3BU

e-mail: info@smokestack-books.co.uk

www.smokestack-books.co.uk

ISBN 9781739772246

Smokestack Books
is represented
by Inpress Ltd

Contents

Preface

Welcome to this second volume of clerihews, a verse form described previously in *The Call of the Clerihew* as 'the limerick's shorter, smarter sibling'. We managed to avoid being sued by any of the celebrities and public figures whose reputation we annihilated in that first volume, so we have decided to chance our arm with a further selection. You'll be glad to know that they are just as scurrilous and scathing as the first batch.

If somehow you missed out on that first volume and are new to the form, we hereinunder repeat the information we included for your edification last time round:

The clerihew was invented as a poetic form by Edmund Clerihew Bentley, a novelist and journalist writing as EC Bentley. His 1905 book *Biography for Beginners* introduced the clerihew to the world and was followed up in later years by *More Biographies* and *Baseless Biographies*. Bentley died in 1956 after authoring some moderately successful detective novels, but it is the verse form that bears his name that cements his place in literary eternity.

The clerihew form is governed by some simple rules:

It must be four lines long
The rhyme scheme is AABB
Rhymes should be tight
Meter may vary across the four lines
The first line must be the name of the person about whom the clerihew is written

As in the previous volume, our poets address the lives, achievements, and reputations of hundreds of both well-known and esoteric figures from a variety of fields. Watch in awe as the poets perform outrageous feats of rhyme and poetic timing along the way, with no thought of their own safety or standing amongst their fellow poets. Marvel at their skill, technique, and commitment as they use light verse to go in heavy.

Since the publication of *The Call of the Clerihew* we've noted a slight resurgence in popularity of the form; *Private Eye* magazine featured a few topical clerihews, and questions on the form appeared on the quiz shows *University Challenge* and *Only Connect*. A friend of the editor now uses the clerihew with children in a Primary School in the North of England – surely a matter of urgent concern for Ofsted inspectors?

As with the previous volume, material for this book was assembled from responses to a series of prompts offered to a community of clerihew devotees on Facebook over several years. This second volume completes the task of bringing these minor poetic gems to the public's attention; our work here appears to be done. Once again, we are indebted to the 70 or so contributors for their enthusiasm and generosity in supporting this book.

Andy Jackson & George Szirtes
September 2022

Actors

Peter O'Toole
Felt a bit of a fool
When, instead of 'Lawrence of Arabia',
He said 'Abhorrence of Labia'.

Tom Deveson

Ellen Burstyn
Was at her worst in
The Exorcist. Despite all the slime,
She had a devil of a time.

Andy Jackson

John Gielgud
Loved Dr Feelgood
And appeared in *Sergeant Bilko*
Along with Wilko.

George Szirtes

Rin Tin Tin
Found it hard to keep his resentment in;
Lassie
Was more classy.

Andy Jackson

Elizabeth Taylor
Never married Norman Mailer
So they avoided the news heading:
'THEIR FIFTEENTH WEDDING'.

Tom Deveson

Steve Busciemi
Always plays characters that are samey.
It would be good
If just for once he wasn't a hood.

Andy Jackson

Harrison Ford
When terminally bored
Would try to go to sleep
By counting electric sheep.

George Szirtes

Robert de Niro,
A 70s hero,
Has well-deserved mockers
Since *Meet the Fockers.*

Adam Horovitz

James Robertson Justice
Said 'A crust is
All an actor can hope for, and that
Is not enough for Sir Lancelot Spratt.'

Andy Jackson

Mel Gibson
Is less subtle than Ibsen.
Henrik satirises conventional views;
Mel blames the Jews.

Tom Deveson

Nicolas Cage
Is now at the stage
Where his career, in summation,
Is just one long Elvis impersonation.

Andy Jackson

Leonard Nimoy
From being a little boy
Harboured dark fears
Of men with pointy ears.

Andy Jackson

Louise Brooks
Was blessed with looks.
John C Reilly?
Perhaps less highly.

Andy Jackson

Buster Keaton
Can't be beaten
(So Harold Lloyd
Is null and void).

Andy Jackson

Gina Lollobrigida
Could not have been rigider
In those days it was more wunderbar
Than Wonderbra.

Peadar O'Donoghue

Yul Brynner
Had rabbit for dinner.
He said, 'To be fair,
I'd rather have hare.'

Joe Williams

Cary Grant
Kept his maiden aunt
At arm's length, saying 'I find her weird
And people think she's my beard.'

Adam Horovitz

Bela Lugosi
Is a fella you'd go see
To experience the vernacular
Of *Count Dracula*.

Rachel Rooney

Christopher Lee
On a killing spree
Would face an inevitable crushing
From Peter Cushing.

Adam Horovitz

Charlton Heston
Didn't keep his vest on.
It was easy to concur
He played Ben Him not Ben Her.

Tom Deveson

Tom Cruise,
Had he taken up booze,
Would have issued an apology
For the Scientology.

Adam Horovitz

Scarlett Johansson
Had see-through pants on
In the opening scene of *Lost in Translation*,
Which, of course, received a standing ovation.

Rachel Rooney

Fred Astaire
Had a big house near Bel Air,
So big, he took in lodgers,
Though not Ginger Rogers.

Simon Williams

Jude Law
Has a romantic flaw.
First he says, 'This is it!'
Then he announces a split.

Tom Deveson

Kevin Bacon
Was the point from which measurements were taken
To assess the fame of any Hollywood hero.
His own rating: an unmatched zero.

David Hill

Mae West
Seemed pretty impressed
With the hidden charms
Of concealed firearms.

Rachel Rooney

Oliver Reed
Favoured tweed,
But when in the buff,
A hat was enough.

Robert Fitzmaurice

John Belushi
Was so impossibly louche he
Made Dan Ackroyd
Seem a saint unalloyed.

Adam Horovitz

Jeff Daniels
Kicks spaniels
If he passes them in the street.
It's not deliberate, he just has big feet.

Adam Horovitz

Tony Curtis,
In an attempt to assert his
Reputation for being the world's sexiest male actor,
Applied quite a lot of Max Factor.

Jim Lindop

Humphrey Bogart
Excelled at the rogue art
While Lauren Bacall was willowy and sireny.
The Big Sleep? What irony!

George Szirtes

Johnny Depp
Declared 'That's one small step
For man!' as he stood to peruse
Tom Cruise.

George Szirtes

Lauren Bacall,
Perhaps the best whistler of all,
Is now a lovely old fogey
Like her ex, Bogey.

Barton Young

Telly Savalas
Often went bra-less;
Alan Whicker's
Rarely in knickers.

Andy Jackson

John Thaw
Now you're no more.
Your life has run its course
Leaving no time for remorse.

Andy Jackson

Mae West
Lent her name to an inflatable vest.
Proverbially Errol Flynn...
Well, where would one begin?

Tim Turnbull

Cyd Charisse
(May she rest in peace)
Preferred to dance with Gene Kelly.
She found Fred smelly.

Andy Jackson

Montgomery Clift
Always the Misfit. Get my drift?
The script? He wouldn't learn it. He
Was Here for a while, but he's now in Eternity.

Andy Jackson

Peter Lorre
Viewed little girls as quarry
And chased after them
In *M*.

Andy Jackson

Keir Dullea
In *2001: A Space Odyssey* was heard to say
'Open the pod bay doors, HAL –
You ain't makin' a monkey out of me, pal.'

Andy Jackson

Mads Mikkelsen
I prefer to Jack Nicholson,
Because, though he looks strange,
He shows far more range.

Ian Duhig

Keira Knightley
Started brightly
Being tipped as an Oscar winner
But quickly faded after dinner.

George Szirtes

Anne Hathaway
Followed her path away
From Brooklyn. Sometime in her acting life,
She should play Shakespeare's wife.

Simon Williams

Woody Allen
Drinks tea by the gallon.
His producer Charles Joffe
Preferred coffe.

Robert Lindsay Marcus

Tom Hanks
Said 'Thanks
For the Oscar for *Philadelphia*.
Now I'm off to play someone healthier.'

Robert Lindsay Marcus

Uma Thurman
Entered church for the sermon.
She only went in
'Cos she thought she saw Quentin.

Robert Lindsay Marcus

Clint Eastwood
Joined the priesthood.
The bishop said 'When you're on show
A cassock's fine but lose the poncho.'

Robert Lindsay Marcus

Mick Jagger
Brought to the role of Ned Kelly much of his rock star swagger.
But he couldn't act.
Fact.

Jim Lindop

Matt LeBlanc,
What a twonk.
He's even dimmer
Than David Schwimmer.

Mark Totterdell

Alastair Sim –
Remember him?
He played it with feeling
In Ealing.

Andy Jackson

Carrie Fisher?
I rather wish her
To be remembered as a player
For things other than Princess Leia.

Adam Horovitz

Liam Neeson
Doesn't do it for me, son.
Schindler's List?
Cease and desist.

Andy Jackson

Morgan Freeman,
Your appeal I just can't see, man.
And as for Tom Hanks?
No thanks.

Andy Jackson

Diana Dors
Won loud applause
When she had the bad luck
To mis-spell 'Diana Fluck'.

Tom Deveson

Noël Coward
And Trevor Howard
Had fewer than two wives
In their Private Lives.

Tom Deveson

Robin Askwith
Tackled every acting task with
Gusto. His only gripe?
Not being available for *Confessions of a Randy 1970s*
Archetype.

Andy Jackson

Charlie Sheen
Makes movies that are rarely if ever seen.
People would rather
Watch his father.

Andy Jackson

Dirk Bogarde
Used to work so hard,
Writing memoirs that from cover to cover
Avoided mention of his long-term lover.

Robert Lindsay Marcus

Dame Maggie Smith
Takes the pith
From oranges she's growing.
Where'd you think thith wath going?

Harry Gallagher

Paul Newman
Was the perfect human
To play Butch.
Nathan Lane, not so much.

Heather Fiona Reid

Vin Diesel.
Just a sneeze'll
Make your underwear rustle.
Even his snot's muscle.

Adam Horovitz

George Clooney
Makes women go all swoony,
Much swoonier
Than for Robert Downey Junior.

Mark Totterdell

Jean-Claude van Damme.
95% ham.
The other 5%?
Oh, from somewhere near Ghent...

Adam Horovitz

Christopher Reeve
Just couldn't make me believe
That a man could fly.
Though boy did he try.

Adam Horovitz

Meryl Streep
Is very deep:
She doesn't look like a dachshund,
But she can do the achsund.

Bill Greenwell

Al Pacino
Starred widely, though never appeared in *The Beano*.
Dark-suited Mafia types
Favour horses' heads over black and red stripes.

Beth McDonough

Peter Finch
In the face of setbacks would not flinch.
It was obvious he'd make it
Being mad as hell and not going to take it.

Andy Jackson

Bruce Willis
Knows what acting skill is,
Though this news is surprising
If you've seen *Mercury Rising*.

Robert Lindsay Marcus

Marcello Mastroianni
Was a fan of Reg Varney,
He'd make all sorts of fusses
If he missed *On the Buses*.

Robert Lindsay Marcus

Barbra Streisand
Dines on rice and
Thin air. You go figure
How she never gets any bigger.

Harry Gallagher

Marlon Brando's
Favourite restaurant was Nando's,
But all that peri-peri chicken
Made his waistline thicken.

Mark Totterdell

Sigourney Weaver
In plain-speaking was a believer:
There's no time to be sesquipedalian
When you're battling an alien.

Robert Lindsay Marcus

Jodie Foster
Solved the clues that Hannibal tossed 'er.
But she was much cooler
As Tallulah.

Robert Lindsay Marcus

Sharon Stone
Raised the tone
Of a film that was rather sordid,
For which she is to be applauded.

Robert Lindsay Marcus

Edward Woodward
Bet on a horse in the 3.30 at Goodwood.
Would he see his bet come good?
Oh yes, Edward Woodward would!

Mark Totterdell

Steve Martin
Played the lead part in
The Jerk,
Arguably his finest work.

Joe Williams

Rachel Weisz
Thinks it's rather neisz
Being married to Daniel Craig,
Though he can be terribly vaig.

Mark Totterdell

Warren Beatty
Made an erotic treaty
That only the most elegant necks
Would inculcate sex.

Robert Fitzmaurice

Architects

Sir Christopher Wren
Said 'I'm going to dine with some men.
If anyone wants to know,
Say I'm designing St Magnus-the Martyr, St Stephen
Walbrook, St Andrew-by-the-Wardrobe, St Peter upon
Cornhill and St Mary-le-Bow.'

Mark Totterdell

William Kent
Spent
Much of his time designing pillars
For villas.

George Szirtes

Robert Adam
Was a proper madam
And would get in the most colossal glooms
About the Glasgow Assembly Rooms.

George Szirtes

Donato Bramante
Raised the ante.
His Renaissance was High,
That's why.

George Szirtes

Antoni Gaudi
Wouldn't drive a tasteful black Audi
As modern architects do.
He'd go for a purple Lamborghini with a furry dice or two.

Peadar O'Donoghue

Eugène Viollet-le-Duc
Constantly took
Great care not to be called Le-Duck,
But it stuck.

George Szirtes

Augustus Pugin
Found expensive blue gin
Made him giggle like a spinster
While designing the Palace of Westminster.

Judith Taylor

Inigo Jones
Piled up heaps of stones
To beautify St James's Palace
So Charles II could display his phallus.

Tom Deveson

Norman Foster
Is no impostor.
There's no need to fret:
What you see is - alas - what you get.

Tom Deveson

Sir Clough Williams-Ellis
Set up an Italianate trellis,
Not to mention a white rubber ball
Ready for Patrick McGoohan to make a call.

Graham Mummery

Terry Farrell
Has clients over a barrel.
If they want the building smaller,
He just makes it taller.

Tom Deveson

Mies van der Rohe
Said 'less is more', though
Never to waiters, financers
Or vaudeville dancers.

Robert Fitzmaurice

Walter Gropius
Built copious
Numbers of buildings. He had nous,
Even though his daddy wouldn't buy him a Bauhaus.

Andy Jackson

Le Corbusier
Was choosier
Than most, eschewing tradition
To feed his towering ambition.

Andy Jackson

Frank Lloyd Wright,
Is commemorated, as is only right,
Not by some monstrous carbuncle
But in a song by Simon and Garfunkel.

Jim Lindop

Vitruvius,
Looking at Vesuvius,
Said 'That underfloor heating
Would take some beating!'

Mark Totterdell

Michel de Klerk;
Of his life and work
I don't know much,
Except that he was Dutch.

Mark Totterdell

Erno Goldfinger
Designed the bold finger
Of concrete known as Trellick,
Which survives as a Brutalist relic.

Mark Totterdell

Renzo Piano
Isn't associated with nano-
Structures. It's hard
To avoid his Shard.

Mark Totterdell

Brexit

Nigel Farage
Said, 'Europe? *Quel dommage!*'
Even his French
Exudes a vile stench.

Tom Deveson

Oswald Mosley
Would have watched Farage closely
And deeply admired
The line about 'not a shot fired'.

Adam Horovitz

Theresa May,
But who's to say:
Given the troubles she got,
She may not.

Tim Turnbull

Jean-Claude Juncker,
Arch-debunker
Of baseless euro-myth,
Says, 'Exeunt forthwith.'

Tim Turnbull

David Cameron
Attempted to stammer on,
But after a referendum
Vanished from the agendum.

Andy Jackson

Angela Merkel
Once joined the Magic Circle.
Having made the Greeks vanish
She started on the Italians, the Irish and the Spanish.

George Szirtes

Comedians

Ken Dodd
Often talked to God
As a form of diversion.
It was the Lord's Prayer in the Diddyversion.

George Szirtes

Paul Merton
Didn't study at Girton,
But his Metalwork CSE
Outweighs many a degree.

Tom Deveson

Les Dawson
Though an irresistible force, an
Immovable object stuck in his craw:
The Mother-in-Law.

Andy Jackson

Jimmy Tarbuck
Hasn't raised the bar. Look,
See how his material grates -
Basically just golf and showbiz mates.

Andy Jackson

Frankie Howerd
Found his fame flowered
When he began to witter
About forbidding us to titter.

Tom Deveson

Hale and Pace
Vanished without trace,
After making lots of money
For not being funny.

Tom Deveson

Tommy Cooper:
What a trooper!
What trick could surpass
'Glass, bottle - bottle, glass'?

Andy Jackson

Jimmy Carr
Was bound to go far.
With all his stuff
He couldn't go far enough.

George Szirtes

Jo and Russell Brand!
They must have planned
To appear as one.
Like mother, like son.

George Szirtes

The Marx Brothers
Were funnier than most others,
Though it's a pity
Karl was less witty.

Mark Totterdell

Jack Benny
Told a few jokes, then he
Would tuck his fiddle under his chins
(I do so abhor senseless violins).

Andy Jackson

Peter Kay
Only has to say
'Garlic Bread'
And I'm off me head.

Andy Jackson

Jasper Carrott
Had a parrot
That was trained to tweet
Funky Moped from a lyric sheet.

Grant Tarbard

Tim Vine's
Single lines
Are even more terse
(And funny) than this verse.

Mark Totterdell

Laurel and Hardy
(One skinny, one lardy)
Used to quarrel
Over whether they should be called Hardy and Laurel.

Mark Totterdell

Ronnie Barker –
Criticism made his mood darker.
But Ronnie Corbett
Could absorb it.

Tom Deveson

Tony Hancock;
It's a shame to see a funny man cock
Things up so badly
That it all ends sadly.

Mark Totterdell

The Goodies
Could ease
The grimness of 70s Britain
With a giant fluffy kitten.

Mark Totterdell

Bill Oddie...
...what a body!
Tim Brooke-Taylor?
Hello sailor!

Andy Jackson

Lou Costello?
Splendid fellow!
Bud Abbott, however, was just the comic feed -
The Ernie that Eric was to need.

Jim Lindop

Ernie Wise
Though smaller than Eric in size
Was but one side of a coin.
You can't see the join.

Andy Jackson

Bill Hicks
Kicked against the pricks.
His most outrageous routine? It
Was his 'suck your own cock' bit.

Jim Lawrence

Peter Cook
Re-wrote the book.
Dudley Moore
Watched in awe.

Andy Jackson

Harry Worth
Was a visitant to earth
And performs in the hereafter
To the sound of Martian laughter.

George Szirtes

Max Miller
Would often thrill a
Crowd with filth. You'll find
Most of it was in our mind.

Andy Jackson

Jimmy James
To this nation's shame
Is now completely forgotten, which makes me retch.
Have a look on YouTube for his 'What's in the Box' sketch.

Andy Jackson

Rod Hull
Was rarely dull,
Though Emu could be a little over-hearty,
Trying to be the life and soul of the party.

George Szirtes

The Goons
Were utter buffoons
And their manic laughter
Echoes in the hereafter.

Paul Green

Victoria Wood
Is gone now for good
But any time we need her
We have Barry and Freda.

Joe Williams

Detectives

Miss Marple's
A lot like Ena Sharples:
Both dislike sensation
And both know their station.

Bill Greenwell

Sexton Blake
Is a bit of a fake.
He fills many tomes
Imitating Sherlock Holmes.

Tom Deveson

Inspector Clouseau
Wore a bride's trousseau
With complete apleumb.
He went down a beumb.

Tom Deveson

Charlie Chan?
Me not a fan,
And have many glipes
About such lacial steleotypes.

Andy Jackson

Columbo
Muttered some mumbo-jumbo,
Some half-heard Yeatsian quote:
'I made my song a coat'.

Tom Deveson

Inspector Lestrade,
Down at The Yard,
Is known as 'Inspector Lestumped'
And will shortly be dumped.

Andy Jackson

Precious Ramotswe?
Each plot's way
Too slight,
Though those African settings delight.

Mark Totterdell

Starsky & Hutch
I didn't like much.
Randall & Hopkirk (Deceased)
were British, at least.

Andy Jackson

Starsky and Hopkirk
Decided to stop work:
It was a case of smartness;
They needed new partners.

Bill Greenwell

Jessica Fletcher
You can betcha
Doesn't float my boat.
Watching her is murder (I wrote).

Andy Jackson

The Ellery Queens
Had confused genes.
The writers had the same grandmother,
The detectives were their own brother.

Tom Deveson

Shaft
Was daft
But blacker
Than Cracker.

Andy Jackson

Dixon of Dock Green
Discovered French haute cuisine,
Thus a new phrase was spawned:
Bonsoir, tout le monde.

Tom Deveson

The Keystone Cops
May have been flops,
But made the 1970s Flying Squad
Look like PC Plod.

Tom Deveson

Inspector Barnaby
Said 'How dangerous could this village gymkhana be?'
Which couldn't have been dumber
Considering this was Midsomer.

Mark Totterdell

Sherlock Holmes
Kept scientific tomes.
He said The Non-Compound Chemical ABC
Was elementary.

Simon Williams

Scooby Doo
Wasn't much of a detective, true.
What annoyed me most?
It was always the janitor dressed as a ghost.

Mark Totterdell

Aurelio Zen
Would now and then
Wonder why
So many of the people he met seemed to die.

WN Herbert

Montalbano
Never watched *The Sopranos.*
He solved crimes while swimmin'
And havin' lunch with beautiful women.

WN Herbert

Philip Marlowe
Arrived in Harlow.
He'd been looking for Jean
So it was a crime of the seen.

Robert Fitzmaurice

Marcus Didius Falco
Never said no to an alco-
Holic beverage or nine
When solving crime in the Aventine.

WN Herbert

John Rebus
Caught the 23 bus
Home from the Oxford Bar,
Saying 'Besht not rishk the car.'

Mark Totterdell

William of Baskerville
Took young Adso to task. 'I've ill
Import of that blind monk,
So be chaste when alone in your bunk.'

Robert Fitzmaurice

Sam Spade and Mike Hammer
Might be thought full of glamour,
Or cool,
Though in fact each is a complete tool.

Mark Totterdell

Perry Mason
Took a new case on.
He was keen to
Get to the moment where someone stood up and shouted 'I did it! I did it! I didn't mean to!'

Bill Greenwell

For The Avoidance of Confusion

Gordon Brown
Is not to be confused with Dan – *DaVinci Code* – Brown.
There was nothing sinister
About being Prime Minister.

George Szirtes

George Osborne in *Vanity Fair*
Was selfish, nasty, vain and made you despair.
George Osborne the Tory -
Same story.

Tom Deveson

William Pitt
Suffered a jealous fit.
He had an insatiable hunger
To be the Elder not the Younger.

Tom Deveson

Yeats
Rhymes with plates.
Keats
With pleats.

George Szirtes

Engelbert Humperdinck
Didn't stop to think
Of what Old Engelbert would think of his pseudonym.
Please, would somebody release him?

Andy Jackson

Frankie Valli
Once met Halle
Berry.
She was jolly. He, not very.

Andy Jackson

Frank Skinner
Never had dinner
With Frank Sinatra.
They came from different strata.

Andy Jackson

Bono
Oh no!
Give me laterality
And Edward De.

Rachel Rooney

John Maynard Keynes
Was the man with the brains
Unlike the blokes in the jeans
Who built Milton Keynes.

Anne Berkeley

Francis Ford Coppola
Wrote *How to Be Popular*,
Unlike Pier Paolo Pasolini
Who wrote *How to Be a Meanie*.

George Szirtes

Russ Meyer
In terms of breast portrayal in movies, a player.
Tinto was more a devotee of the ass
Proving that where there's muck, there's Brass.

Andy Jackson

Gretel
Had quite a crush on Sebastian Vettel,
While Hansel
Had an inexplicable fondness for Nigel Mansell.

Mark Totterdell

Lennie Bruce
Had no use
For Angus Lennie.
There wasn't any.

Andy Jackson

Michelangelo
One thing I know
About him, is this:
He's not Michael Angelis.

Andy Jackson

Ken Dodd;
It strikes me as odd
That he is not
The same person as Ken Stott.

Andy Jackson

Elizabeth the First
Was cursed
With not being fecund,
Unlike Elizabeth the Second.

Anne Berkeley

Mr Kipling
Had no time for tippling,
Said 'I work ruddy 'ard
Unlike that lazy bard.'

Robert Fitzmaurice

Mary Stuart, Queen of Scots
Was lots
Less hairy
Than her cousin Bloody Mary.

Sarah Walker

Leonardo Di Vinci
Never met Maeve Binchy.
Had he done so, a different oeuvre
Might have made its way to the Louvre.

Simon Williams

Dr Spock
Was the child-rearing doc,
Not one of the guys
From the Starship Enterprise.

Anne Berkeley

Paul Potts;
What's
Vital to know is, he's not
Pol Pot.

Mark Totterdell

Pope
John Paul will not, I hope,
Be confused with Pope John
Paul II. That was a different one.

Andy Jackson

Mr Fitzwilliam Darcy
Is stylish, elegant and classy.
To say the same of Colin Firth
Excites mirth.

Tom Deveson

Edward Heath
Was no natural leader, hence a brief
Stay in power. Unlike Heath, Ted
Who led bands until dead.

Adam Horovitz

Julius Caesar
Was a Victorian cricketing geezer:
The other formed an unstable sexual trio
With Ptolemy and Cleo.

Tom Deveson

Kim Jong-un
Is a wrong-un,
But then again so was Kim Jong-Il.
This last line was hard to fill.

Robert Fitzmaurice

Steve McQueen
Dominated many a Hollywood screen.
Came back British and younger,
Directing indie pics like Hunger.

David Hill

Jocky Wilson,
You gave us a thrill, son.
Top of The Pops must have been on wacky-baccy
To mistake you for Jackie.

Peadar O'Donoghue

Sigmund Freud
And Lucian Freud
Were related.
Imagine if they'd dated.

Alvin Pang

Russell Brand
Is not to be confused with Dollar Brand,
Later known as Abdullah Ibrahim.
Russ is not him.

George Szirtes

Carl Sagan
Was essentially a pagan.
Françoise Sagan
Left faith to her grande-maman.

Tom Deveson

Iain Crichton Smith
Drew from Gaelic myth;
Iain Duncan-Smith
Should disappear forthwith.

Tom Deveson

Robert Falcon Scott
Should not
Be confused with Robert Edwin Peary. For a start,
They were poles apart.

Mark Totterdell

Philip Larkin
Is not to be confused with Molly Parkin.
The former wrote *Letters to Monica*.
Molly played the harmonica.

George Szirtes

Robert Lowell
Is not to be confused with Amy Lowell
But as for Christ's bowels
I throw in both towels.

George Szirtes

Jane Seymour
(Winsome actress) couldn't be more
Different to Henry the Eighth's bird
(The third).

Andy Jackson

Jerry Lee Lewis
Was heard to ask 'Who is
That idiot with my name hangin' round with Dean Martin?
I fear trouble's startin'.'

Andy Jackson

Katie Price
Is not to be confused with Posh Spice.
Despite what many claim
They are not the same.

George Szirtes

Iain Sinclair
Walks everywhere.
He doesn't like to drive
Unlike Sir Clive.

Deborah Sibbald

John Barry
Would be as happy as Larry
To know his name lives on
In Welsh rugby legend Barry John.

Andy Jackson

David Mitchell
Wrote *Cloud Atlas,* which'll
Suggest he's not the same
As the David Mitchell who appears on every TV panel game.

Mark Totterdell

Jaws
Is not to be confused with *Jaws.*
One had steel teeth
The other was lurking beneath.

George Szirtes

Federico del Sagrado Corazón de Jesús García Lorca.
His name was a corker,
Like a contemporary of his:
Antonio Cipriano José María y Francisco de Santa Ana
Machado y Ruiz.

Sharon Larkin

Duke Ellington
Is not to be confused with The Duke of Wellington.
One was a brilliant jazz musician who played the Harlem
Cotton Club.
The other is a pub.

Jim Lindop

Richard Burton
(Liz Taylor's beau) should not, I'm certain,
Be confused with the translator
Of *The Arabian Nights* and discoverer of the source of the Nile.
He came later.

Andy Jackson

In The Kitchen

Gordon Ramsay
Doesn't give a damn, see.
He is a man with one goal:
To combine profanity with profiterole.

Andy Jackson

Nigel Slater
Will cater
At the drop of a hat.
Just watch that fat.

Robert Fitzmaurice

Michael Winner;
Don't have him to dinner,
Because if you do
You'll have a Death Wish too.

Andy Jackson

The Hairy Bikers
Are they just like us?
No, not very –
They're much more hairy.

Andy Jackson

Delia Smith
Cooks bara brith
With her usual immutable
Instructions: Dried yeast is not suitable.

Anne Berkeley

Keith Floyd
Was easily annoyed
Till he got to the wine.
Then he was fine.

Judith Taylor

Fanny Craddock
Boiled a haddock,
Garnished it with dark green mash,
A dash of Cointreau and a stray eyelash.

Kristina Close

Nigella Lawson
Never forgot to put the sauce on,
Which kept us looking
But not at her cooking.

Mark Granier

Heston Blumenthal
Said 'There's no room at all
For simple food in MY damn fridge.
Now, who wants a Plutonium Sandwich?'

Andy Jackson

Paul Hollywood;
True, he makes jolly good
Bread
But it's gone to his head.

Andy Jackson

Greg Wallace
Sought solace
From main courses that weren't any good
By pigging out on the pud.

Mark Totterdell

Marco Pierre White
Got a terrible fright.
A French surname was forsaken
Because 'Blanc' was already taken.

Andy Jackson

Clement Freud
Tried to avoid
Cooking bulls' phalluses
Because of psychoanalysis.

Tom Deveson

Graham Kerr
He made the camera purr.
But it was a dodgy scallop
That made this gourmet gallop.

Grant Tarbard

Libertines

Giacomo Casanova
Liked to get his leg over
When in his prime,
Which was most of the time.

Andy Jackson

Charles the Second,
When Nell Gwyn beckoned,
Was glad to be of use:
'Thank you, Nell. Lovely juice!'

Tom Deveson

Charles Baudelaire
Was wont to declare:
'Jeanne Duval rocks!'
Pity about the pox.

Tom Deveson

The Marquis de Sade
Said, 'It's a bit – ahem – hard.
I don't want kisses.
I want infinite orifices.'

Tom Deveson

Pierre Ambroise François Choderlos de Laclos
Wrote about what he shouldn't know.
Most of it concerned copulation,
Which thankfully wasn't lost in translation.

Andy Jackson

Russell Brand
Would often make a stand.
You have probably heard that story,
His gland of hope and glory.

Robert Fitzmaurice

Oscar Wilde
Was unfairly reviled,
Not for his theatrical arts
But for his private parts.

Tom Deveson

Fatty Arbuckle
Was shaped like a cheese truckle
But was a varlet
With a starlet.

Bill Greenwell

Jacqueline du Pré
Liked to play
With a fellow
As well as a cello.

Bill Greenwell

Zsa Zsa Gabor
Liked to score,
But looking back
Couldn't keep track.

Bill Greenwell

Byron
Had a constant desire on
Even when nibbling
A sibling.

Bill Greenwell

The Duchess of Argyll
Made men smile
When they were bedless
And posing headless.

Bill Greenwell

Mae West
Powdered her breast
As the clock struck seven.
Time to go to heaven.

Robert Fitzmaurice

Micky Rourke
Loved sticky pork.
Barbecued on wood
It was finger-licking good.

Robert Fitzmaurice

John Wilkes
Liked courtesans in silks,
But preferred them to undress
And wear even less.

Tom Deveson

Leopold von Sacher-Masoch
Is an absolute wazzock,
Venus infers.
Leopold submissively concurs.

Mark Totterdell

Aleister Crowley
Wasn't holy
In the least,
The beast.

Mark Totterdell

Don Giovanni
Grabbed a quick sarnie,
But was so focused on thrusts
He had no time for the crusts.

Robert Fitzmaurice

Literary Figures – 14th Century

Geoffrey Chaucer
Wrote coarser
Tales than would've been allowed
By today's PC crowd.

Andy Jackson

Literary Figures – 17th Century

Robert Herrick
Was the kind of cleric
Who gave less attention to prayer
Than to ladies' underwear.

Tom Deveson

John Donne
Enjoyed a long run
With his erotic stage show
'Before, Behind, Between, Above, Below.'

Tom Deveson

Literary Figures – 18th Century

Colley Cibber
Might have been a fibber
A crook and a skiver,
But if you identified him you got a fiver.

Michael Rosen

William Blake
Can be opaque;
To me it's apparent
It's OK to be not transparent.

Michael Rosen

Literary Figures – 19th Century

Had Thomas Hardy
Discovered Bacardi
Jude the Obscure
Might have been a lot less dour.

Adam Horovitz

Mark Twain
Laughed like a drain.
Oscar Wilde
Merely smiled.

George Szirtes

Lewis Carroll
Was gleefully shooting fish in a barrel
When in a fit of malice
He shot poor Alice.

George Szirtes

Charlotte Brontë
Cried 'Cheers! Slainte! Sante!
Of damp this parsonage smells –
No wonder we've turned to Bells.'

Judith Taylor

Mary Ann Evans
Said 'Good Heavens!
If I publish *Adam Bede*
Under the name of Eliot, they'll read.'

Sarah Walker

Charles Dickens
Said, 'The plot thickens...'
He was writing, *Edwin Drood*.
To be continued...

Michael Rosen

Victor Hugo
Yeah, there you go,
With your great oeuvre which is
Now on stage as *Les Mis*.

Michael Rosen

Literary Figures – 20th Century

Edgar Rice Burroughs
Ploughed several literary furrows,
And though he wrote a lot
Is now The Man That Time Forgot.

Andy Jackson

John Steinbeck
Wrote misery in every line. Heck,
Even Doris Lessing
Was less depressing.

Andy Jackson

Dennis Wheatley
Wrote fast but neatly.
It was satanic trash
Which made mountains of cash.

Sarah Walker

Antoine de Saint-Exupéry
Wrote stuff which was super. He
Has been very famous since
The Little Prince.

Sarah Walker

Philip K Dick
Was very quick
To realise when he fell asleep
That he was dreaming of an electric sheep.

Graham Mummery

Arundhati Roy
Has a name designed to annoy
Anyone not arty-farty.
What's wrong with Roy Arundhati?

George Szirtes

Alexandr Isayevich Solzhenitsyn
Should have put more funny bits in
The works he sent abroad:
Think Hattie Jacques in *Cancer Ward*.

Tim Turnbull

Norman Mailer
Liked the odd sailor
Such as Jean Genet.
He was funny that way.

John Muckle

George Bernard Shaw
Wrote 250,000 letters or more.
There's no record of him having writer's cramps.
I would like the value of the stamps.

Simon Williams

Fyodor Dostoevsky
Was taking a brisk stroll down the Nevsky,
Whiling away the time
Between punishment and crime.

George Szirtes

Bertolt Brecht
Knew what was echt.
As you'd expect
It was when talking of *Verfremdungseffekt*.

Michael Rosen

Graham Greene
Is no has-been.
He took second place
In a competition to write with his grace.

Angela Topping

Ted Hughes
Sang the blues
When he'd had a laugh
With Sylvia Plath.

Carole Bromley

JB Priestley
Was far from beastly,
He had the balls
To write *An Inspector Calls*.

Carole Bromley

Maud Gonne
Told Yeats it was not on,
And he had the same result
When he tried Iseult.

Matthew Francis

Harper Lee
Appeals to me,
Her book was fun
But she stopped at one.

Carole Bromley

Harper Lee –
You've written a second book? Dearie me!
While that's terrific
It's hardly prolific.

Andy Jackson

DH Lawrence
Had an abhorrence
For women with the slightest imperfections.
Pity we never heard their reflections!

Harry Gallagher

Albert Camus
Is better than you.
None of you guys
Have a Nobel Prize.

Joe Williams

Jean Plaidy
Was an amazing lady
Who took much of the mystery
Out of history.

Sue Barnard

Muriel Spark
Found writing a lark,
But it was a surprise
She never got a Booker Prize.

Francis Moorcroft

Jean Rhys
Never had any peace.
She took a voyage in the dark
And ended up sleeping in a park.

Deborah Sibbald

Jeffrey Archer
Anticipated a new literary departure.
He said 'O for a Muse of Fire!'
The Muse said 'Get lost, Liar!'

Tom Deveson

Willie Russell
Flexed a muscle
And for a moment looked surly,
Then out popped Rita and Shirley.

Harry Gallagher

James Joyce
Had a unique voice,
Although his vocabulary
Upset the constabulary.

Mark Totterdell

George Orwell
Wrote *Nineteen Eighty-Four*, well
Aware that the date
Was 1948.

Mark Totterdell

Arthur Miller
Complained 'What a killer!
Marilyn's bum is so very goosable,
How will I ever finish *The Crucible*?'

Mark Totterdell

Ernest Hemingway
Didn't quite write the Fleming way,
But I've read feminist analyses that show
They were both reprehensibly macho.

Robert Lindsay Marcus

Gertrude Stein
Wrote lots of very fine
Books. Nobody can understand 'em
So you can just read bits at random.

Susan Jordan

Kazuo Ishiguro
Was very pro-Euro:
After having his say,
He was named Remainer of the Day.

Robert Lindsay Marcus

W Somerset Maugham,
On particularly good form,
Wrote *Of Human Bondage* way way way
Before EL James wrote *Fifty Shades of Grey*.

Mark Totterdell

Arnold Wesker
Said, '*Est-ce que*
Vous voulez
Voir ma pièce au sujet de Soupe de Poulet?'

Tom Deveson

Will Self -
Will. Self.
Name
And nature the same.

Tom Deveson

Don DeLillo –
I suggest you read his books with a pillow.
You'll keep
Dropping asleep.

Tom Deveson

Angela Carter
Had three desiderata –
The pelagic, the camouflagic
And magic.

Tom Deveson

Eugene O'Neill
Would have a broader appeal
If his plays went the other way:
A Long Night's Journey into Day.

Tom Deveson

Anthony Powell
Was a kindly soul,
But he'd rip out your bowel
If you called him 'Powell'.

Tom Deveson

F Scott Fitzgerald
Never drove a Triumph Herald.
His car of choice
Would be a swanky great big yellow Rolls Royce.

Mark Totterdell

Iris Murdoch
Loved dandelion and burdock,
But she could never persuade AS Byatt
To try it.

Mark Totterdell

e e cummings'
works are worth a few thumbings,
but they wouldn't half read better
with the occasional capital letter.

Mark Totterdell

Dodie Smith,
According to myth,
Wrote the first draft of *The Hundred and One Dalmatians*
Featuring Alsatians.

Mark Totterdell

Julian Barnes
Wrote True-Blue British Boys' Own Ripping Yarns –
OK but with ideally a
Little less Francophilia.

Tom Deveson

Marcus J. D. Salinger
Has no serious challenger
As distiller of the essence
Of tortured adolescence.

Robert Lindsay

Stephen King
Wrote the ring-bing-bing-bing-bing
Chorus bit
For Crazy Frog's greatest hit.

Tim Turnbull

Vladimir Nabokov
Made the singer from Abba cough
When he told her about the size
Of his collection of butterflies.

Robert Lindsay Marcus

Gabriel Garcia Marquez
Liked to wander around starquez.
No-one wanted to see him nude
So he wrote *One Hundred Years of Solitude.*

Robert Lindsay Marcus

Kurt Vonnegut, Jr.
Came up with plots that could scarcely have been loonier;
When he thought of one that he couldn't work out
He'd pretend it was by Kilgore Trout.

Robert Lindsay Marcus

Ouida
Wrote novels that today have barely a reader.
There is a statue of her opposite a Tesco Metro
In Bury-St-Edmunds. How retro!

Jim Lindop

Arthur Ransome
Was most awfully handsome
And rather good at sailing
Except when the wind was galing.

Susan Jordan

Harold Pinter
Quipped to Santa one winter,
'Your reindeer, Mr. Claus, is
Notable for its long paws   es.'

Robert Lindsay Marcus

Ezra Pound
Somehow never got around
To putting Esperanto
Into a Canto.

Christopher Reid

Flann O'Brien
Found it very tryin'
Folk wouldn't distinguish between
Him and Myles naGopaleen.

Judith Taylor

Thomas Mann
Faced a ban
By the Nazis. 'It's because he is decadent' said Hermann
Goering.
My history teacher thought it should be 'Because he's so
boring.'

Graham Mummery

John Wyndham
Came up with some working titles, then binned 'em
As probable failures:
'The Chicken Wakes'. 'The Midwich Cockapoos'. 'The Day of
the Dahlias'.

Mark Totterdell

Literary Figures – 21st Century

Hilary Mantel,
As far as anybody can tell,
Is likely to win
Just about any literary prize she's entered in.

Mark Totterdell

Dan Brown
Throws another manuscript down,
But we have grown weary
Of his conspiracy theory.

Andy Jackson

Lee Child
Is rightly reviled
For his remorseless creature
Jack Reacher.

Andy Jackson

Donal Ryan
Is reduced to cryin',
Because he can't remember
The thing about December.

Brian Kirk

EL James
Shames.
Shifty grades of wahay
Coming your way.

Robert Fitzmaurice

Peter Carey
Writes kind of modern fairy
Tales, where things feel slightly alien
Though clearly Australian.

Mark Totterdell

Audrey Niffenegger
Is a lucky beggar.
With the power to stop clocks,
She's a temporal paradox.

Andy Jackson

Iain McEwan?
I'm liking his new 'un.
Mark Haddon?
His new 'un's a bad 'un.

Andy Jackson

Robert Galbraith
Is merely a wraith,
He's no one that I can see,
Just a casual vacancy.

Brian Kirk

John Le Carré
Had to tarry
Hard and be wily
To repeat the success of George Smiley.

Graham Mummery

'Joseph O'Connor.'
'Yes. Your Honour?'
'You are charged with beautiful writing.'
'Guilty, Your Honour. I find it exciting.'

Jim Lindop

Zadie Smith
Is becoming a myth
Puffed by the inflation
Of her fans' adulation.

Tom Deveson

Jonathan Coe
Is a good man to know
If you fancy some grub
At *The Rotters Club*.

George Szirtes

Graham Swift
Was disinclined to drift.
See what it says in your name?
Now do the same.

George Szirtes

Donna Tartt
Is a good place to start.
But William Boyd?
Avoid.

Andy Jackson

William Boyd
Ain't always one to avoid.
Any Human Heart
Is better than owt by Donna Tartt.

Jim Lindop

William Boyd?
His reputation is destroyed
By measuring him against Donna;
He's a goner.

Andy Jackson

William Boyd
Is most annoyed
That some think of him as a lemming
After writing as Ian Fleming.

Graham Mummery

Lionel Shriver
Was a terrible driver.
Every trip was potentially her final.
We need to talk about Lionel.

George Szirtes

Eleanor Catton;
Her novel would flatten
And squash you all right,
If dropped from a height.

Mark Totterdell

Orhan Pamuk
Sleeps in a hammock.
Did so in full sun, the berk.
Now he really is a well-red Turk.

Robert Fitzmaurice

AS Byatt
Was attacked in a riot
And leading the rabble
Was Margaret Drabble.

Tom Deveson

Sarah Waters
Was known in certain quarters
For her velveting and fingering.
That reputation's lingering.

George Szirtes

Aravind Adiga
Is eager
To point out that his name
Doesn't rhyme with the novel that brought him fame.

Mark Totterdell

Edward St Aubyn
Met Colm Toibin...
(Do they actually rhyme? Oh heck,
I'm going to have to check).

Mark Totterdell

JM Coetzee
Seldom makes notes. He
Keeps it all in his head,
Which should be taken as read.

Andy Jackson

Yann Martel
Treats his groupies rather well.
If one should catch his eye
She's bound to get a piece of his Pi.

Andy Jackson

James Kelman
Is not a well man
And must find all that swearing
A bit wearing.

Andy Jackson

Roddy Doyle
Has a novel on the boil.
O God Almighty and his Holy Company of Saints and Lord
Jaysus Christ and his Blessed Virgin Mother!
Please, not another!

Tom Deveson

JK Rowling
Did not approve of disembowelling
Or of any operation
Involving defenestration.

Always excepting Simon Cowell,
Whom she would cheerfully disembowel.
No ifs, no buts.
She hated his guts.

George Szirtes

George RR Martin
Can't keep himself from startin'
Yet another narrative thread.
It usually ends with someone dead.

Sarah Walker

Literary Figures & Poultry

Charles Dickens
Kept chickens.
His henhouse was bleak.
He had a miserable streak.

George Szirtes

Boz
Would often go out bird-watching in Oz.
He was last seen getting lairy
With a Cassowary.

Andy Jackson

William Thackeray
Loved quackery.
His pedigree ducks were the talk of the season –
With good reason.

Katy Evans-Bush

Gottfried Benn
Didn't raise a single hen.
He saved his breath
For cancer, bodily fluids and death.

Tom Deveson

Ezra Pound
Thought it was sound
To lecture ducks on Social Credit.
But they quacked and simply didn't geddit.

James Sutherland-Smith

Tony Harrison
Said, 'There's just no comparison
Between pursuing Aeschylus's phantom
And feeding my bantam.'

Tom Deveson

Louis MacNeice
Let you fondle his geese.
John Betjeman?
He wouldn't let you, man.

Andy Jackson

John Cooper Clarke
Thought it a lark
To always have poultry around.
Evidently Chickentown.

Andy Jackson

Movie Characters

Tommy DeVito
Was rarely seen incognito.
He loved his mother, and money.
What do you mean that's funny? Funny how? How is that
funny?

Andy Jackson

Yoda
Owed a
Lot to Frank Oz.
The master he was.

Andy Jackson

Sam Spade
Was never afraid.
Best not to talk
About Phil Fork.

Mark Totterdell

Sam
Said 'Damn!
I'm doomed to play *As Time Goes By*
Until I die.'

George Szirtes

Charles Foster Kane
Was heard to complain:
'Millions of bucks, power, two wives in bed –
But I want my sled!'

Tom Deveson

Norman Bates
Stockpiled hates,
And you could never be certain
What was behind the shower curtain.

Robert Fitzmaurice

Harry Lime
Spent his time in crime, them grime and slime.
He didn't dither
At the sound of the zither.

Tom Deveson

Ellen Ripley
Never drinks, never gets tipply.
She's so ripped she can chuck her
Nemesis out of the air lock, motherfucker.

Simon Williams

Clarice Starling
Was Hannibal's darling.
He was having a friend for dinner;
Let's hope it was Michael Winner.

Andy Jackson

Jack Torrance
Warrants
A place in a clerihew.
'Heeeeere's Johnny!' Oh, it's you.

Andy Jackson

Keyser Soze
Knows he
Exists. Or not,
Which is the essence of the plot.

Andy Jackson

Maximus Decimus Meridius
Found Commodus to be perfidious
And not nearly as touchy-feely as
Marcus Aurelius.

Andy Jackson

Rhett Butler
Could have been subtler,
And his emphasis was distinctly ham,
In 'Frankly my dear, I don't *give* a damn'.

Simon Williams

Travis Bickle
Ain't worth a nickel.
Am I talkin' to you, dear?
Well, there ain't nobody else here...

Andy Jackson

Vito Corleone
Looked up from his minestrone,
Saying 'Normally this tastes fine,
But I seem to have a horse's head in mine.'

Andy Jackson

Mrs. Danvers
Was not apt to canvas
Opinion or brook inter-
Ference from the new Mrs. De Winter.

Bill Greenwell

The Lone Ranger
Was never in danger,
Not with Tonto
So pronto.

Bill Greenwell

Sugar Kane
Hurrying for the train
Moved various things –
'Like Jell-O on springs.'

Tom Deveson

Beowulf
Opened up a gulf
Between the Old English epic verse
And Ray Winstone's cockney curse.

Sarah Walker

Calvera
Said, 'It could be numerically fairer.
You kill me plus another twenty or more.
I only kill four.'

Tom Deveson

Billy Liar
Finds his fantasies misfire
So he doesn't get to do the biz
With Liz.

Tom Deveson

The Invisible Man
Had a plan
To find an invisible lady
And make an invisible baby.

Peadar O'Donoghue

Juror #8
Turned around that young man's fate
But with the fishes he could have been swimmin'
For the other court had 12 angry women.

Peadar O'Donoghue

Alien;
All toothy and scaly and
Bursting through shirts.
No wonder John Hurts.

Mark Totterdell

Spiderman
Has often tied a man
With spider-thread, which would *so* be a
Reason for arachnophobia.

Mark Totterdell

Mr Chips
Licked his lips.
Teaching languages it was no surprise
He went crazy for French fries.

Robert Fitzmaurice

Philosophers

Ayn Rand
Was roundly panned
For condemning the Collective
But she was just being Objective.

Andy Jackson

Jean Baudrillard
Is the worst philosopher by far.
If you want it done proper
Ask Popper.

Andy Jackson

Martin Heidegger
As played by Arnold Schwarzenegger
Eviscerated Time
And turned his Being to crime.

Adam Horovitz

Thomas Aquinas
Wrote tracts of incredible dryness;
But it was a bit of a bummer
That he died so soon after finishing his Summa.

Mandy Macdonald

Galen Strawson
Said to Nigella Lawson:
'Is identity located in the brain
Or in cocaine?'

Tom Deveson

GE Moore
Had students rolling on the floor:
'No tutorial today, folks!
Just some Ethics Girl Jokes!'

Tom Deveson

Socrates
Was never at ease
When Xanthippe
Got lippy.

Brian Joyce

Plato
Was great. Oh
Seek him out in your browsers,
But don't expect trousers.

Robert Fitzmaurice

BF Skinner
Was a winner.
It infuriated him
When anyone said behaviour was a whim.

Grant Tarbard

Thomas Kuhn
Changed paradigms too soon.
He said, 'It's a real drag
But Popper had a brand new bag.'

Tom Deveson

Steven Pinker
Said, 'I am, therefore I'm a thinker',
Showing, of course,
He'd put Descartes before the horse.

Tom Deveson

Willard Van Orman Quine
Said, 'Teaching logic? Fine!'
But more than work in college, he
Liked wrestling with normative epistemology.

Tom Deveson

Gilbert Ryle
Said, 'Television isn't my style.'
He thought he had seen
A Ghost in his Machine.

Tom Deveson

Ludwig Wittgenstein
Was seen to repine.
'Why the long face?'
'The world is everything that is the hopeless case.'

Tom Deveson

Jacques Derrida
Had an early career that was varied. A
Football career sucked
So he taught himself to deconstruct.

Andy Jackson

Blaise Pascal
Was a bit of a rascal
Who misspent his youth
In search of mathematical truth.

Andy Jackson

John Locke
Had a bit of a shock
When his tabula rasa
Was hit by a laser.

Robert Fitzmaurice

AJ Ayer
Felt it unfair
That he had to recount his life story
Feeling that such knowledge should be *a priori*.

Andy Jackson

Emmanuel Kant
May rhyme with pant or want.
It doesn't much matter
But my money's on the latter.

George Szirtes

John Duns Scotus
Wished to denote us
As possessing a 'thisness'.
Such was his business.

Sarah Walker

Peter Abelard
Found it very hard
To focus on salvation in his cell
When Heloise was kneeling there as well.

Sarah Walker

Jean-Paul Sartre
Could bore the arse off you for hours at cafés in Montmartre.
Simone de Beauvoir, however,
Never.

Jim Lindop

Parmenides
Wrote at speed. His
Horror of space
Dictated the pace.

Robert Fitzmaurice

Benedict de Spinoza
Knows a
Lot about God, all
There is to know. I, however, know sod all.

Andy Jackson

David Hume
Was thrown out of the Metaphysicians' Room
With undue force.
He'd failed their Induction course.

Tom Deveson

Richard Rorty
Said, 'I'll teach something naughty.
The contingent world may not exist,
So let's just get pissed.'

Tom Deveson

Judith Butler –
Her writing could be subtler.
It's not informative
To bang on incomprehensibly about the performative.

Tom Deveson

Peter Sloterdijk
Went on strike
Refused to read Socrates
And put Kant on deep freeze.

Karen Margolis

Bertrand Russell
Pulled a muscle
But wouldn't say where
To AJ Ayer.

Judith Taylor

Karl Popper
Never wore a topper.
If this statement were reliable
It would be falsifiable.

Sarah Walker

Diogenes of Sinope
Looks pretty ropey
And his behaviour's canine.
Call me a cynic, but I think that's fine.

Rachel Rooney

Jacques Lacan,
The post-structuralists' man,
Played with mirrors and symbolism.
Well, what d'you expect from post-modernism?

Karen Margolis

Soren Kierkegaard
Pondered long and hard
On being, consciousness and God.
The neighbours thought him odd.

Sarah Walker

Gotthold Ephraim Lessing
Said 'I'm not messing
But this problem is a bitch.
I will call it Lessing's Ditch.'

Sarah Walker

William of Ockham
Liked to shock 'em
With philosophical shaving:
It's all those unnecessary assumptions I'm saving.

Graham Mummery

Pythagoras
Can no longer stagger us.
We have so much hotter news
Than the square on the hypotenuse.

Matthew Francis

Sigmund Freud
Experimented with an alkaloid
That is now forbidden
Because it does your Id in.

Matthew Francis

Heraclitus
Declared everything flows, and whether he's right is
Debatable,
Because he's so terribly untranslatable.

Mandy Macdonald

Politics

Anthony Charles Lynton Blair
Is in despair.
Public office left him unsatisfied;
He'd have rather been beatified.

Tim Turnbull

Jeffrey Archer
Enjoys a regular departure
With women of the night
(And now that's been proven I can say that without fear of
prosecution, right?).

Andy Jackson

Boris Johnson
The sexiest blonde since Mick Ronson
Physique of a Greek God and skin like a Vermeer
(I may have gone a bit overboard here).

Andy Jackson

Kelvin McKenzie
He's at it again, see...
Evil Misanthrope or just a grotesque act?
He should be sacked.

Andy Jackson

Sir John Major
Sent a message on his Prime Ministerial pager:
'Urgent. Ultra-Highest Priority. Top Secret. Hurry.
I need a hot curry.'

Tom Deveson

Benjamin Disraeli
Declined to meet his sovereign daily.
Yet when at last he came to yield,
He was created Beaconsfield.

Alfred Corn

Silvio Berlusconi
Wielded his baloney,
And calling for bunga bunga
Slobbered, 'Younger. Younger'.

Robert Fitzmaurice

Aneurin Bevan
On reaching heaven
Knew no constraints.
He democratised God, and all the saints.

Adam Horovitz

General de Gaulle
Found himself in a haulle
When he asked the French to help him *dans son guerre*;
Most of 'em didn't cuerre.

Jim Lindop

Margaret Thatcher
Met with no one to match her
Determination to have her own way
(Aside from her pal, Pinochet).

Mark Granier

Clement Attlee
Flatly
Refused to have Churchill as a mate,
Being too busy sorting out the Welfare State.

Andy Jackson

Anthony Eden
Found himself needin'
A miracle, and knew his
Time was over after Suez.

Andy Jackson

Herbert Asquith
Said 'Germany's strength is a crass myth,
We'll give 'em what for!'
Thus, the Great War.

Grant Tarbard

Oliver Cromwell
Went down a bomb. Well,
Not with everyone, especially Mike,
The chap who stuck his head on a spike.

Robert Fitzmaurice

Alec Douglas-Home
Had a sense of impending dome
And asked his Chief Whip 'What d'you know
About John Profumo?'

Andy Jackson

Oswald Mosely
Changed his clothes. He
Hopped and skipped parties
From Labour to Nazis.

Adam Horovitz

Geoffrey Howe
Thought, 'What a cow!'
It was no great leap
After Thatcher called him a sheep.

Adam Horovitz

Harold MacMillan;
Supermac or Supervillain?
I'm sure there are two sides to the story,
But a Tory is a Tory is a Tory.

Andy Jackson

Giuseppe Garibaldi;
When Italian reunification called, he
Answered. He decided to risk it
But his methods took the biscuit.

Andy Jackson

General Galtieri
Was fairly
Sure the Malvinas
Were Argentina's.

Robert Fitzmaurice

Paul Dacre
When he goes to meet his Maker
Lord Satan in Hell
Will complain about the smell.

Martin Rowson

Niccolò Machiavelli
Was on the side of hell, he
Thought it realpolitik
To manipulate the weak.

Jane Baston

Edward Heath
Had magnificent teeth
And was very proud
Of his Morning Cloud.

Sue Barnard

Benito Mussolini
Enjoyed being seen, he
Always wanted to be looked at, only less so
When inverted at the Esso.

Brian Kirk

Jeremy Corbyn
Shows how much crap you can absorb in
A life devoted to politics –
'Forward to Nineteen-Seventy-Six!'

Tom Deveson

Harold Wilson
Said, *The Waste Land* gives me a thrill, son.
And even better, don't mock it,
Is the Pound in my pocket.'

Tom Deveson

BoJo the Clown
Has let everyone down.
Have we ever had a more sinister
Prime Minister?

Sue Barnard

Sir Stafford Cripps
Used to extract the pips,
Whereas Iain Duncan Smith
Just takes the pith.

Tom Deveson

Peter Mandleson
Should have had handles on.
Let's face it, it's the only way
You could stop him spinning away.

Harry Gallagher

Jeremy Hunt
Was quite upfront.
A&E not working? It will
If we stop being ill.

Carole Bromley

Enoch Powell
And his racist growl
About bloody rivers
Gave me the shivers.

Andy Jackson

Nigel Farage
(Judging by his visage)
Was the result of a snog
Between a tortoise and a frog.

Sue Barnard

The former 2nd Viscount Stansgate, the Right Honourable
Anthony Neil Wedgwood Benn
Never reached Number Ten,
But as he rose to fame
Bits kept dropping off his name.

Tom Deveson

James Keir Hardie
Was Scottishly mardy
From a child-in-the-pits start he
Gave workers their own party.

Ruth Aylett

Nelson Mandela,
Remarkable feller,
Forgave those who took half his life.
Would be a saint if it weren't for his wife.

Harry Gallagher

Liz Truss:
Can she be trusted? Discuss.
My advice is
Don't trust Liz.

Andy Jackson

Pop Music – the Beatles

Ringo Starr
Couldn't play the guitar
But he made amends
With quite a lot of help from his friends.

Tom Deveson

Paul McCartney
Had a heavy heart, 'n he
Said 'I'm off to greater things'
Inexplicably thinking that thing was Wings.

Andy Jackson

George Harrison
Said, 'There's no comparison
Between taking Pattie Boyd to bed
And being dead.'

Tom Deveson

Pete Best
Had a short rest
He felt a bit of a fool
When he found Ringo had nicked his stool.

Andy Jackson

Billy Preston
Was deemed best on
Keyboards. They asked me
But I said 'Let It Be'.

Andy Jackson

George Martin
Played only a small part in
The Beatles' success. Just things
Like producing all the records, playing the piano and writing
arrangements and accompaniments for brass and strings.

Tom Deveson

Pop Music – the 60s

Chas Chandler
Could handle a
Beer or three,
For an Animal was he.

Andy Jackson

Sandie Shaw
Dislocated her jaw
When she tried to sing
'Puppet on a Supersymmetric Multidimensional String'.

Tom Deveson

Keith Moon
Turned up to the studio one day with a tune.
But Roger Daltrey
Considered it paltry.

Andy Jackson

Dave Dee
Said 'It's all about me'.
'That's rich'
Countered Dozy, Beaky, Mick & Tich.

Andy Jackson

Bob Dylan
Is still an
Icon. But Tiny Tim –
What happened to him?

Andy Jackson

Simon Dee
Wondered, 'What's become of me?
Think of what might have been!'
But that was long off-screen.

George Szirtes

Keef
Nearly came to grief
While playing the opening riff to *Gimme Shelter*
On a helter-skelter.

Jim Lindop

Tiny Tim,
Tall and slim,
Regretted his pass
At Mama Cass.

Robert Fitzmaurice

Lulu
Blew
The cobwebs away when she sang *Shout*.
But I've no idea what it was about.

Jim Lindop

Pop Music – the 70s

Benny
Is at it again. He
Is reading a stack of Swedish porn
With Bjorn.

Frida
Surprised many a reader
When she appeared in such magazines without her sweater
With Agnetha.

Andy Jackson

Jethro Tull,
In the lull
After inventing the seed drill, planned
A new career as a prog rock band.

Mark Totterdell

Gary Glitter
Looked like a cross between The Tin Man and a gas fitter.
Every time he sang
We thought, 'Don't want to be in HIS gang!'

Jim Lindop

Bonnie Tyler
Was not much of a smiler
And looked even glummer
Than Donna Summer.

Andy Jackson

David Bowie
Was well in the know. He
Could tell you things about Suzi Quatro
But he'd better not, though.

Andy Jackson

Smokie
Made a demo disc of *The Hokey-Cokey*.
For, in the 70s, there was never any doubt
That that is what it was all about.

Jim Lindop

Leo Sayer,
(5 foot 2 inches, including his hair,)
Was often caught
Short.

Jim Lindop

The Clash
Said 'We're here to smash
Self-indulgent prog rock'. I'd guess
They were referring to Yes.

Andy Jackson

Mud?
No good.
Showaddywaddy?
Bloody shoddy.

Andy Jackson

Neil Young
Bit his tongue.
He couldn't expunge
The title 'Grandfather of Grunge'.

Bethany W Pope

Terry Jacks,
Needing to relax,
Spent a season in the sun
But didn't have joy, didn't have fun.

Andy Jackson

Tony Orlando
Would often go commando
For which, though not strictly a crime,
I feel he should do some time.

Andy Jackson

Elkie Brooks
Was much loved by cooks
But it can't have been her pork in brine,
Must have been the lilac wine.

Robert Fitzmaurice

The Bee Gees
Give me the heebie-jeebies.
Where in the libretto
Does it indicate so much falsetto?

Andy Jackson

Jean-Michel Jarre
Said to me *'Qui sont ces mannequins là-bas?'*
I said 'Ya daft berk,
That's Kraftwerk'.

Andy Jackson

Squeeze
Disbanded, then reformed. These
Days play *Up the Junction*
At weddings/bar mitzvahs/other functions.

Shauna Robertson

Gloria Gaynor
Hired a personal trainer
To prepare for her fight
With Barry White.

Andy Jackson

Brotherhood of Man
I wasn't a fan,
So don't bother saving any kisses
For me, or the missus.

Andy Jackson

The Osmond Brothers;
You mean there were others?
I know about Donny, sure,
But FIVE more?

Andy Jackson

Stevie Wonder
When feeling under
The weather, found
Solace on Higher Ground.

Shauna Robertson

Queen
Spawned many a mondegreen
Like that one in *Bohemian Rhapsody*
'The Ellesmere pub has a treble buttered side for meeee!'

Andy Jackson

Johnny Rotten
Will never be forgotten;
Caustically witty,
And neither vacant nor pretty.

Andy Jackson

Paul Simon
Was nicknamed Rhymin',
Unfortunately by someone at the time,
Who didn't understand rhyme.

Simon Williams

The Ramones
Were all skin and bones
Owing to their diet of coke,
Speedballs and a smoke.

Andy Jackson

Pop music – the 80s

Bob Geldof
Never held off,
I think you'll find,
From speaking his mind.

Mark Totterdell

Simon Le Bon
Has fixations on
A girl whom he pursues with brio
Whose name, apparently, is Rio.

Andy Jackson

Luke Goss
Formed Bros
Not only with his brother Matt,
But with another fella, though no-one remembers that.

Andy Jackson

Bono,
In conversation at a Fund-raising Charity Ball with Yoko Ono,
Heard her state that U2
Were poo.

Jim Lindop

Black Lace
Are looking to gain a place
In the Rock'n'Roll Hall of Fame. They won't.
'Agadon't, don't don't'.

Andy Jackson

Shakin' Stevens
Put all his chips on Evens,
But the croupier said with a grin
'This ole house will win.'

Robert Fitzmaurice

Bananarama
Turned everything into a drama;
Robert Palmer
Was invariably calmer.

Andy Jackson

Billy Joel
Dug himself into a hole
When he slept with a fan;
Not such an innocent man.

Andy Jackson

Whitney Houston
Never read *A la Recherche du Temps Perdu* by Proust on
Tour;
It would have made her snore.

Mark Totterdell

Hall & Oates
Lost my votes
When they decided not to call
Themselves Oates & Hall.

Andy Jackson

Marti Pellow,
A charming fellow,
Who had always wanted a pet,
Bought three fish called Wet, Wet and Wet.

John Duckworth

Bobby Brown
Wears a worried frown.
The Thompson Twins
Prefer cheesy grins.

Andy Jackson

George Michael,
Enjoyed to cycle,
Helmets, he didn't need 'em,
He much preferred his freedom.

John Duckworth

Kajagoogoo
Never sang *Chattanooga Choo Choo*.
Swing
Wasn't their thing.

Mark Totterdell

OMD
OMG!
Frantic
New Romantics.

Simon Williams

Gary Numan
Looked not quite human.
Are friends electric? I guess,
In his case, probably yes.

Mark Totterdell

The Jam
Ate Spam
As redress
For rifling three large bowls of Eton Mess.

Simon Williams

Adam Ant
Wasn't as adamant
As Adam Adamant
Even with the Ants.

Simon Williams

Julian Cope
Might reform The Teardrop Explodes, their fans hope,
Except these days he's turned all mythic
And Neolithic.

Mark Totterdell

Elvis Costello
Refuses to mellow
And has grown a beard.
It's worse than we feared.

Martin Figura

Morrissey
Is not a bad writer. Nor is he
Devoid of ardent fans constantly quoting his stuff.
Seems fair enough.

David Hill

Trevor Horn
Was sad and forlorn.
Despite noisily proclaiming his art
Was still the owner of a lonely heart.

John Duckworth

Phil Oakey
Has hair that looks Blokey
On the right, and yet
On the left, effeminate.

Martin Figura

Joe Dolce;
Whatsamatta he? Call me bolshie.
But I wish someone would
Shaddimupp for good.

Andy Jackson

Pete Burns,
By studying, learns
That Schrödinger's cat, Clive,
Is unknown to be dead or alive.

John Duckworth

Shane MacGowan
Liked a drink now an'
Then, and then, and then, and then.
Same again?

Mark Totterdell

Tony Hadley;
It's not that he sang badly,
But, to cut a long story short,
He wasn't really my sort.

Andy Jackson

Chris Rea
Was good to hear
On old cassettes –
How fast one forgets.

Karen Margolis

Chris de Burgh?
URGH!
That's enough said
About *Lady in Red*.

Mark Totterdell

Madonna Ciccone
Was constantly branded a phoney.
Jaded, she was heard to say
"I really need a holiday".

John Duckworth

Status Quo
In the 80s had no idea which way their music should go.
So, to avoid getting bored,
They learned another chord.

Jim Lindop

Belinda Carlisle.
The look. The smile.
But Rick Astley?
Simply ghastly.

Andy Jackson

Tina Turner
Deserved to earn her
Status as an icon that endures to this day;
Icon Tina Turner, you might say.

Mark Totterdell

Kylie
Was regarded highly
For her teeth. The Pogues'
Teeth were awful compared to Ms Minogue's.

Mark Totterdell

Band Aid:
Nobody has made
It to Number 1 any faster
Than this sticking plaster.

Rachel Rooney

Cyndi Lauper
Woke up from a state of torpor
Trying to remember exactly what she'd done.
The girl shouldn't have had so much fun.

Mark Totterdell

Bucks Fizz;
Your name is
One I'd sooner
Not hear said by Spooner.

Mark Totterdell

Irene Cara
Was a massive star a
While ago with *Fame*.
Now, ironically, she's 'Irene what's-her-name?'

Mark Totterdell

Mel and Kim;
Were they him and him, her and him,
Her and her or him and her?
I'm not sure what they were.

Mark Totterdell

Grace Jones
What spectacular bones.
You could pull up to her bumper
Unless you were Russell Harty in a jumper.

Robert Fitzmaurice

Sting
Shouldn't sing.
It's a breach of the peace.
Call the Police.

Mark Totterdell

Kate Bush
Was asked: 'Oy, mush,
Ain't you 'ad your fill
Of running up that hill?'

Adam Horovitz

Billy Idol
Didn't wear a bridal
Gown, though he was heading
For a white wedding.

Mark Totterdell

The Stone Roses'
Decade closes
On an eponymous high – but they go cold
After *Fool's Gold*.

Adam Horovitz

The Fall?
I can't recall
All the changed line-ups-ah
Formed when Mark's in his cups-ah.

Adam Horovitz

Luther Vandross
Came across
As a man
Whose name described his music if you left out 'Luther Van'.

Mark Totterdell

Iggy Pop
Never knew when to stop,
Or if he ever knew,
Stopping wasn't something he'd ever do.

Mark Totterdell

Puppets

Keith Harris
Said 'Don't you love Paris?'
Orville the Duck
Said 'I don't care one way or the other.'

Tom Deveson

Muffin the Mule
Is against every rule,
And, as has been attested,
Will get you arrested.

Mark Totterdell

Andy Pandy
Was notoriously randy
And would, now and then,
Make improper advances to The Flowerpot Men.

George Szirtes

Looby Loo
Sniffed glue
And was always ready
For a bit of Teddy.

George Szirtes

Peter Brough
Murmured: 'You're really hot stuff',
Which made Archie the wooden dummy
Start shouting for his mummy.

Tom Deveson

Miss Piggy
Lit up a ciggie.
Oh what a damnable
Shame she was flammable!

Mark Totterdell

Lord Haw Haw
Had strings, sure,
But unlike most puppets, William Joyce
Had a choice.

Adam Horovitz

Fozzie Bear
Won't be a millionaire.
It's uneconomic
Being a furry comic.

Tom Deveson

Professor Yaffle
Was my prize in a raffle.
I said 'For me, you can shove him,
Let Emily love him.'

Andy Jackson

The Flowerpot Men,
Every now and then,
Talked to a weed
And smoked it, indeed.

Jim Lindop

Kermit
Had to apply for a permit
For his solar-powered composting latrine.
It's not easy being green.

Mark Totterdell

Lord Charles
Snarls
And keeps a talon
In Ray Alan.

Adam Horovitz

The Swedish Chef
Was a trifle deaf
Which led to his main vocal quirk,
Chiefly 'Hurdy-blurdy-blurk-blurk-blurk'.

Andy Jackson

Lamb Chop
Came from a shop.
He really could rock,
Though made from a sock.

Bethany W Pope

Nookie Bear
Used to be welcomed everywhere
But is now a bitter divorcee,
Citing Roger de Courcey.

Andy Jackson

Fingermouse
Used to be on in every house,
His popularity growing by the minute,
Though Yoffy had a hand in it.

Andy Jackson

Gordon the Gopher
Now works as a chauffeur
And takes *This Morning* with Phil
As a bitter damned pill.

Adam Horovitz

Big Bird,
It could be inferred,
Plucked and roasted would be plenty
For a family of twenty.

Mark Totterdell

Commander Shore
At Marineville parties was a complete bore.
Troy Tempest knew, as he nodded and cowered,
Nothing would happen in the next half hour.

Simon William

Captain Scarlet
Dated many a starlet,
As the source of female adulation
For his supermarionation.

Andy Jackson

The Clangers
Eschewed cosmic *Sturm und Drang*, as
The acceptable characterisation
Of an alien civilisation.

Andy Jackson

Mr Punch:
The crocodile stole his lunch,
But cold revenge is all in the news,
Just look at his crocodile shoes!

Peadar O'Donoghue

Pinky and Perky
Had views that were quirky.
They said: 'It's abundantly clear
That Bacon wrote Shakespeare.'

Tom Deveson

Bert
Threatened to dish the dirt
On Ernie,
Who promptly hired an attorney.

Mark Totterdell

Sooty
Measured only a foot. He
Was a bit of a creep.
I preferred Sweep.

Andy Jackson

Basil Brush
Filled me with a rush
To blow the stupid puppet to his doom.
Boom boom.

Andy Jackson

Thunderbirds were GO
(Tracy Brothers, Brains and co)
But they weren't as F-A-B
As Lady Penelope.

Sharon Larkin

Religion

Buddha
Gave the old coulda-shoulda-woulda
A non-attached KERPOW!!!
And lives in the Now.

WN Herbert

Shiva
Is an over-achiever –
Creator of everything from the microbe to the giant sequoia
But also the Destroyer.

Tom Deveson

Vishnu
Wished to
Keep everything ticking over on the planet, or
Put another way, be a cosmic janitor.

Andy Jackson

Ali
Went to Bali
To check the beaches
For modesty breaches.

Karen Margolis

Mary Baker Eddy
Declared our health would be quite steady
If we'd all get past our defiance
And read the texts of Christian Science.

Alfred Corn

Noah
Could have aimed lower
And rid the ark of faeces
By having just one of each species.

Andy Jackson

Doubting Thomas
Went down a bomb as
An atheist figurehead,
By rejecting the undead.

Andy Jackson

Yahweh
Said 'My way
Tends to be mercurial
Hence my angels Gabriel, Raphael and Muriel.'

George Szirtes

Judas Iscariot
Fingered the lariat.
Let down by the silver bung
He could at last be well hung.

Robert Fitzmaurice

Adam
Said 'Madam,
Correct me if I'm wrong,
But one of us is speaking with forked tongue.'

Andy Jackson

Eve
Was naïve.
It's an elementary mistake
To listen to a talking snake.

Mark Totterdell

Jesus
Sees us
Whatever we do.
Can that be true?

Mark Totterdell

Jesus
Frees us
From guilt at what we do or say
(But he's still watching anyway).

Andy Jackson

Herod Agrippa
Was feeling chipper.
'Bring me John the Baptist's head on a platter,
Deep fried in batter!'

George Szirtes

Lot
Married a woman who was not
Easy to convince,
And they haven't looked back since.

Andy Jackson

Lazarus
Said 'What's all the fuss?
Of course I'm a bit whiffy;
I'm just your regular stiffy!'

Robert Fitzmaurice

Abraham
Gave his neighbour a ham,
Saying 'My diet
Forbids it, but you try it'.

Mark Totterdell

Jonah
Was no moaner.
Even when swallowed he said 'I'm
Having a whale of a time.'

Andy Jackson

Saul
Became Paul
On the road to Damascus?
A tall story if you ask us!

Mark Totterdell

Jehovah
After the Creation was over
Said, 'That's done, thank the Lord.
Now back to the drawing board.'

Tom Deveson

Joseph
Knows if
The truth comes out about his coat not being that nice
He'll have to deal with Sir Tim Rice.

Andy Jackson

Moses
Said, 'It'll be no bed of roses.
I beat Him down to ten kinds of sin
But Adultery's still in.'

Tom Deveson

Joshua,
Gosh, you were
A minor character, or so I learn,
But small prophet, quick return.

Andy Jackson

Isaiah
Satisfies school-children's desire
For smut and worse:
Thirty-sixth chapter, twelfth verse.

Tom Deveson

The Apostle Luke
Became a doctor by a fluke.
One day he found a surgical lancet
And thought he should chance it.

George Szirtes

Abel
Should have worn a label
So Cain could wait
Until his Kill-by Date.

Tom Deveson

Matthew, Mark, Luke and John
Went on and on and on and on
About Jesus and stuff.
Stop it, that's enough!

Mark Totterdell

Satan
Would often create an
Unholy situation,
Usually involving temptation.

Andy Jackson

Herod the Great
Said 'Slaughter every last neonate'.
Ok, so he was insecure, but still,
That does seem like overkill.

Andy Jackson

Daniel
Said 'That's too big for a spaniel.
That's more of a roar than a yelp.
Help!'

Mark Totterdell

The Four Evangelists –
Their stories emerge from the mists.
They're amorphous and eerie
Like post-modernist narratological theory.

Tom Deveson

Jezebel
Told Elijah to go to Hell.
She said, 'You make me cross.
Prophet? You're a dead loss.'

Tom Deveson

Delilah?
It was easy for Samson to rile her,
Particularly as he preferred to work on his pecs
Than have sex.

Andy Jackson

Pontius Pilate
Turned a blind eye. 'Let
Him die if you're eager.
Now, pass the Swarfega.'

Andy Jackson

Goliath the Philistine
Attributed his decline
To the fact that he'd intoned
'Everybody must get stoned.'

Tom Deveson

The Holy Ghost
Made this proud boast:
'I'm a Doctor of Divinity
After reading Theology at Trinity.'

Tom Deveson

Ruth
Said, 'God's truth
I'll choose
The Jews'.

Karen Margolis

Solomon
Wasn't the solemn one.
He didn't write the Lamentations.
He had other preoccupations.

George Szirtes

Jacob and Esau,
How these things seesaw!
I'll have to keep reading to see which of the twins
Wins.

Mark Totterdell

Ezekiel
Found his roof was leaky. 'Hell!'
He said, 'I'll ask God to fix it.'
'*Ipse fac!' Dominus dixit.*

Jim Lindop

Melchizedek?
Who the heck?
I think I'll say something witty
Like he plays on the wing for Manchester City.

Peadar O'Donoghue

Mary
Oh Mary, quite contrary,
How did that baby grow?
She replied, 'I'm buggered if I know!'

Peadar O'Donoghue

Methuselah
Would bamboozle a
Gerontologist. 'I feel fine'
He'd say, until the age of 969.

Mark Totterdell

Rebekah
Enjoyed Isaac's pecker.
Still, they had to wait many a year
For the twins to appear.

Karen Margolis

Religion & Quantum Physics

Albert Einstein
Said 'This is a fine time
To tell me that it's possible for something to travel faster than light.
I bid you goodnight.'

Andy Jackson

Isaac Newton
Replied, 'That's a cute 'un,
And is bound to keep them busy.
One up to Izzy!'

George Szirtes

Steven Hawking
Said 'It's got everyone talking
But they'll soon get weary
Of Albert's theory.'

Andy Jackson

Jehovah
Declared Game Over.
Let There Be Light!
Good Night!

George Szirtes

God
Thought it odd
That there were so many articles
About indefinite particles.

Andy Jackson

The Son
Said no-one
But me
Is worth the definite article 'the'.

George Szirtes

The Holy Ghost
Doesn't like to boast
But when he goes to Mass
He's a gas!

Andy Jackson

Royalty

Lady Jane Grey
Was made queen one day,
And it all went great
For the following eight.

Joe Williams

Charles the Third
Has only just occurred.
One can only wonder
If it will be a grotesque blunder.

Mark Totterdell

Henry Tudor
Was louder and lewder
Than most other kings, so no real shocks
When he died of the pox.

Tim Turnbull

The Prince of Wales
Rarely hails
From the Principality.
He too suffers from creeping mortality.

George Szirtes

Edward II
Reckoned
Isabella was a bit of a joker
Until she said 'Let me introduce you to my leetle poker.'

Andy Jackson

William I
Was called all sorts of names. Worst
By far, while its currency lasted,
Was 'William the Bastard'.

Andy Jackson

William the Second
Was widely reckoned
(Till the arrow hit)
To be a bit of a git.

Sarah Walker

George VI
Had mixed
Reviews when heard to sing
'G-G-God Save The K-K-K-King'.

Andy Jackson

Ivan The Terrible
Had clothes that were just too unwearable
Together! I mean, would you wear a pink Cossack hat
With that?

Jim Lindop

Marie Antoinette
Said, 'Let them eat baguette!'
While dressed as a peasant,
The outcome wasn't pleasant.

Grant Tarbard

King Zog
Said, 'What's past is prologue.
I've bade fame adieu.
I'm now a crossword clue.'

Tom Deveson

Henry VIII
Was easy to hate.
His taste for death
Quite took my breath.

Bethany W Pope

James the First
Was the worst
At counting, and thus it was fixed
That he was James the Sixth.

Grant Tarbard

Catherine of Braganza
Deserves much more than a stanza,
But this clerihew
Will just have to do.

Mark Totterdell

Harold Hardrada
Should have tried harder.
At Stamford Bridge he tried several ways
(But it's difficult to get a result at Chelsea these days).

Andy Jackson

King Philip II of Spain,
A right royal pain,
Declared 'I'm harder
Than Liz'. A claim not proven by his armada.

Simon Williams

Henry Beauclerc
Was not a jerk
But when the White Ship was lost he
Became rather frosty.

Sarah Walker

Ethelred the Second
Stayed put, whoever beckoned.
He was so full of dread, he
Got called The Unready.

Judith Taylor

George the Fourth
Headed north
Where he felt no guilt
About wearing the kilt.

Judith Taylor

Diana
Said, 'I plan a
Dig at the monarchy that really smarts.
I'll say I'm queen of people's hearts.'

David Hill

The Empress Matilda, Regina Romanorum,
Behaved with decorum.
But when the English crown was stolen by her cousin
She uttered obscenities about him by the dozen.

Sarah Walker

John Balliol
Was set up to fail. They all
Thought he was a waste of space,
And said it to his face.

Edward Longshanks
Said to Balliol 'Thanks
For being such a softie. You can keep your head;
I'll have Scotland on a plate instead.'

Andy Jackson

Henry the Angevin
Tried to begin
His reign and not wreck it.
It was just a shame about Becket.

Sarah Walker

The Prince of Wales
Consorts with snails.
He says: 'This is not at my leisure,
But is my only erotic pleasure.'

Robert Fitzmaurice

The King of Siam
Considered himself the big I Am,
Which is fair enough because
He was.

Mark Totterdell

Roddy Llewellyn
Said, 'My secret? Not tellin'.
I simply can't.
(But I had a small part in *Charley's Aunt*).'

Tom Deveson

Edward Longshanks
Procured a thong thanks
To 'Ye High & Mighty'.
'Strewth, the best shop in Blighty!'

Robert Fitzmaurice

Good King Wenceslas
Said 'Fix those fences! Last
Thing I want is some peasant fool
Stealing my winter fuel.'

Mark Totterdell

Queen Victoria?
I won't bore ya
With tales about her love of bed and booze -
She would not be amused.

Andy Jackson

Charles the Fat
Said, 'Don't call me that!
But at least I'm not called
Charles the Bald.'

Tom Deveson

Malcolm Canmore
Moved to Stanmore.
Sitting in Dunfermline toun
Was getting him doun.

Judith Taylor

King John
Went on and on
Insisting it was bosh
To say he'd lost his crown in the Wash.

Judith Taylor

King Cnut;
Two letters back to frnot
And you'd
Have something really rude.

Mark Totterdell

Henry the Fourth (Part One)
Is really about his son,
And much the same is true
Of Henry the Fourth (Part Two).

George Szirtes

King Farouk
Liked to go to the souk
Eating lots of food
And looking at pictures of women in the nude.

Peadar O'Donoghue

Prince Rupert of the Rhine
Was a swine:
He and Boye would pillage
Any roundhead town or village.

Tim Turnbull

Bonnie Prince Charlie
Had two hits with Bob Marley:
'Over the sea, no cry'
And 'No woman to Skye'.

Tom Deveson

Prince Harry of Wales
Has hair as red as ruby ales.
So has Capt James Hewitt, when polo-playing.
#Justsaying.

Simon Williams

Queen Catherine the Great
Was disinclined to wait.
Her annexation of Lithuania
Was a part of her mania.

George Szirtes

Sophie, Countess of Wessex
Said 'The only way ISN'T Essex.
There's a way that's better by far;
Wessex, yah!'

Mark Totterdell

Richard the Third
Finds it absurd
That his name, uniquely among his species,
Is rhyming slang for 'faeces'.

Andy Jackson

Sporting Legends

Kenny Dalglish
is impossible to pastiche.
His finishing was spectacular,
Less so his Scots vernacular.

Andy Jackson

Dick Fosbury
Was very
Keen to ensure his spirits didn't drop
After each new flop.

Andy Jackson

Learie Constantine
Was a connoisseur of wine:
Freddie Trueman
Was a home brew man.

George Szirtes

Eddie Waring
Was always kind and sharing
And would let anybody come
To join him in the scrum.

George Szirtes

Ferenc Puskas
Was fond of buskers
But Dixie Dean
Was less keen.

Andy Jackson

Jose Mourinho
Reckons himself quite the bambino
But he's no Bill Shankly
Frankly.

Andy Jackson

Geoff Hurst –
To Germans accursed;
To Englishmen near divinity
For his holy Wembley trinity.

Tom Deveson

Tom Finney –
His earnings were skinny,
Fourteen quid a week –
But his gifts were unique.

Tom Deveson

Sebastian Coe –
His career lost its glow
When he ruined the story
By becoming a Tory.

Tom Deveson

WG Grace
Had a hirsute face;
Umpires were afeared
Of his bristling beard.

Bill Greenwell

Jesse Owens
Spent the '36 Olympics showin'
Hitler and everyone in the place
How to run a master race.

Andy Jackson

Muhammad Ali
Is keeping a tally,
Saying 'If you talk to ME
It's Muhammad A-li'.

Andy Jackson

Bjorn Borg
Was cool as a morgue
But an angry John McEnroe
Was more prone to whacking, though.

Andy Jackson

Princess Anne
Attacked a fan
Who asked, with force,
'Are you the rider or the horse?'

Tom Deveson

Bradley Wiggins
Would confuse Henry Higgins.
His French – off the Beaufort Scale.
His English – Maida Vale.

Tom Deveson

Arnold Palmer
Was quite a charmer.
Tiger Woods
Was not as good.

Andy Jackson

Diego Maradona
Said 'I wanna
Come clean. That hand wasn't divine,
It was mine.'

Andy Jackson

Linford Christie
Is sadly missed. He
Was faster than the bunch,
Plus you could see where he kept his lunch.

Andy Jackson

Shane Warne
Was often torn
Between getting up early
And Elizabeth Hurley.

Andy Jackson

Beth Tweddle
Was bound to 'medal';
She'd the best of all names
At the Olympic Games.

Mark Totterdell

Marvin Hagler
Was prone to waggle a
Finger before throwing his fist;
Truly the pugilist's pugilist.

Andy Jackson

George Best
Never second. The rest
Was noise –
And one for the boys.

Robert Fitzmaurice

George Worst
Was cursed
By his name,
And therefore never achieved sporting fame.

Mark Totterdell

Lionel Messi,
Yes he
Is a genius, and no slouch,
But he ain't no Peter Crouch.

Andy Jackson

Gordon Banks –
Let us give thanks
For that skilful and brave
Save.

Tom Deveson

Mike Brearley
Commented severely
On a logical hiatus
In Geoff Boycott's Tractatus.

Tom Deveson

Phil 'The Power' Taylor
Knew his arm was getting frailer
When he had a stinker
Against Paul 'The Pillock' Tinker.

Andy Jackson

Denis Law
Said, 'Life has a tragic flaw,
Running the whole way through –
England 4, Germany 2.'

Tom Deveson

Nobby Stiles
Suffered agony from his piles
When he sat on his false teeth
And bit himself underneath.

Tom Deveson

Jocky Wilson
Said 'Life after darts still gives me a thrill, son
But the one thing I don't miss, though,
Is Eric Bristow.'

Andy Jackson

Stirling Moss
Became very cross
When he was beaten in the Grand Prix
By an OAP in a 2CV.

Tom Deveson

Lester Piggott
Took command of a frigate.
He didn't find it relaxing;
He found it very taxing.

Tom Deveson

Sir Alex Ferguson
Spent summers flipping burgers on
The griddle at Burger King.
He would say 'Yes' to anything.

Andy Jackson

Baron de Coubertin
Had a Greek-inspired plan.
But there is no historical record at all
That Heracles ever played Beach Volleyball.

Andy Jackson

Torvill and Dean
Ordered drinks in the canteen:
'Whisky neat, twice,
No ice.'

Tom Deveson

Nadia Comaneci
Was, in her later years, a dissolute wreci,
Driving fast cars
And hanging around bars.

Andy Jackson

AP McCoy
Would often enjoy
At the end of each day
A sugar lump and nosebag of hay.

Andy Jackson

Roger Bannister
Said to a fan 'Is there
Any reason why, once in a while,
One shouldn't go the extra mile?'

Andy Jackson

Chris Brasher
Said 'I'll race yer
For a quid'. Not Roger's style;
He ran a mile.

Andy Jackson

Christopher Chataway
Has now gone thataway,
Still in good shape
And breasting the final tape.

Tom Deveson

David Beckham
Was born in Leytonstone not Peckham,
But wherever you're born you can transcend it
If you just learn to bend it.

George Szirtes

Ian Botham
Has his faults; for those who don't know them,
He had a reputation
For excessive recreation.

Andy Jackson

Dennis Lillee
Thought it was silly
When he was caught by Peter Willey
Off Graham Dilley.

Tom Deveson

Alistair Cook,
After the debacle of the Ashes series, took
To sessions with Goochie, where he'd thrive
On comments like, 'Never judge a Cook by his cover-drive.'

Jim Lindop

Merv Hughes
Was keen to abuse.
Batsmen at the crease
Wished he would cease.

Andy Jackson

Freddie Trueman
Licked his lips as the new man
Took guard. His first ball
Was aimed straight at his wherewithal.

Jim Lindop

Michael Holding
Never took to scolding
Opponents. He'd silently take their breath
Away bowling like whispering death.

Graham Mummery

Jon Snow;
I never know
Which one to choose –
Fast bowler, *Game of Thrones* or *Channel Four News*.

Andy Jackson

Don Bradman
Said, 'You must be a madman
If you think you'll ever score
An average of Ninety-Nine Point Nine Four.'

Tom Deveson

Yelena Isinbayeva
That was the name that they gave her
With the aid of a pole she could soar
Five metres, and a bit more.

Joe Williams

Strange Bedfellows

Harold Macmillan
Did a gig with Bob Dylan.
The audience went mad
When they sang, 'You ain't ever had it so bad.'

Tom Deveson

Margaret Thatcher
Was never seen together with the Child Catcher.
No-one is to blame –
They're one and the same.

Andy Jackson

General Custer
Should never have hooked up with Prince Buster.
While Buster was windin' up his waist
The General took one in the face.

Andy Jackson

Igor Stravinsky
Never dated Monica Lewinsky,
Didn't offer to make her a star,
Nor misuse his cigar.

Tom Deveson

Helena Bonham-Carter
Once employed Harald Sakata
To put up a marquee
(Bit of an Odd Job if you ask me).

Andy Jackson

Susan Boyle
Was never immortalised by Sir Arthur Conan Doyle.
Why remains a mystery
Now that they're both history.

Andy Jackson

Arthur Askey
Never met Harold Laski.
Both were pretty bright sparks,
But meant something different by Marx.

George Szirtes

Germaine Greer
Met Richard Gere
Who told her she was pretty.
She let him live out of pity.

Kristina Close

Bertrand Russell
Had an underdeveloped comedy muscle
Till Russell Brand
Took him in hand.

Andy Jackson

Rosa Parks
Once entered a legal arrangement with Groucho Marx.
Not such a crazy idea, because
There ain't no sanity clause.

Andy Jackson

Winston Churchill
Never met Julie Burchill.
History is full of these
Sad missed opportunities.

George Szirtes

Charles Saatchi
Was besotted with Liberace,
A regular fella –
Unlike Nigella.

George Szirtes

Vladimir Putin
Was a fan of Dorothy Tutin.
He loved her Cecily,
Albeit messily.

George Szirtes

Henrik Ibsen
Said to Guy Gibson
With all the force he could muster:
'You can't write worth a damn, buster!'

Tom Deveson

Winston Churchill
Met Julie Burchill.
He talked of fighting on beaches.
She wrote biting features.

Adam Horovitz

Boris Yeltsin
Was once propositioned by Vanessa Feltz in
Red Square, for a bet.
His answer? '*Niet*'.

Andy Jackson

The Third Reich

Adolf Hitler
Had one ball littler
Than the other, if indeed he had that ball
At all.

Mark Totterdell

Rudolf Hess
Is someone I could not like less.
Heinrich Himmler
Is somewhat similar.

Andy Jackson

Hermann Goering
Had an aim that was unerring.
He thrashed Goebbels at snowballs and was rough
With Hitler, but he quit when the Goering got tough.

Jim Lindop

Joseph Goebbels
Had a fetish for gerbils.
He was sincere
Saying, 'I want to be like Richard Gere.'

Grant Tarbard

Virtuosi

Jacqueline du Pré
Went out to play
While Daniel Barenboim
Stayed at hoim.

Andy Jackson

Antonio Stradivarius
Longed to be gregarious
But was thought of as a loner
In Cremona.

Andy Jackson

Yo-Yo Ma
Is the best cellist by far.
It's quite a thing,
The way he goes up and down on a string.

Mark Totterdell

Herbert von Karajan
Conducted an ice cream van
That played in perfect stereophonic.
On nights away from the Berlin Philharmonic.

Graham Mummery

Andre Previn
Changed his name to Kevin
After Eric and Ernie slew
His credibility by calling him Mr. Preview.

Graham Mummery

Nigel Kennedy?
Can someone tell me, when is he
Going to stop with that goofy grinning
And get on with his violinning?

Andy Jackson

Vanessa-Mae
Was a prodigy in her day,
But those times have passed.
Now she's going downhill fast.

Mark Totterdell

Niccolo Paganini
Is the Genie
Of the Violin, but don't let Niccolo
Near a piccolo.

Mark Totterdell

Mstislav Rostropovich
Could easily detect a drop of pitch.
It was usually Georg Solti
Who was faulty.

Andy Jackson

Lang Lang
Is fond of a gangbang.
His sister Ling Long
Prefers a sing-song.

Andy Jackson

Murray Perahia
Was a terrible lahia,
Though Glenn Gould
Was invariably fould.

Andy Jackson

Yehudi Menuhin;
Now there's a genuine
Virtuoso,
Who makes the rest look so-so.

Mark Totterdell

The Editors

Andy Jackson
White, male, Anglo-Saxon,
Writes poems not so much shiny as steady.
Don't we have enough of those already?

George Szirtes
Started publishing poetry in his early thirties,
And of all poets born in Budapest
Was once voted 17th best.

Andy Croft
Initially scoffed
At the idea of a book celebrating the clerihew
Then published two.

Sue Barnard
Worked darn hard
On both volumes, correcting mess
Before they went to press.